Measurements & Metrics:

3rd Grade Math Workbook Series

Speedy Publishing LLC
40 E. Main St. #1156
Newark, DE 19711
www.speedypublishing.com

Customary Units

1 yd = 3 ft	3 tsp = 1 Tbs
1 ft = 12 in	16 Tbs = 1 cup
1 fathom = 6 ft	1 cup = 8 oz
1 mi = 5, 280 ft	1 pt = 2 cups
1 acre = 43,560 ft^2	1 qt = 2 pt
1 lb = 16 oz	1 gal = 4 qt
1 T = 2000 lb	1 gal = 231 in^3
	1 ft^3 = 7.48 gal

1. 30 in = ______ ft ______ in

2. 2 gal = ______ qt

3. 40 in = ______ ft ______ in

4. 11 yd 2 ft = ______ ft

5. 3 qt 3 C = ______ C

6. 5 C = _____ qt _____ C

7. 3 pt = _____ qt _____ pt

8. 32 oz = _____ lb _____ oz

9. 5 pt = _____ qt _____ pt

10. 7 C = _____ pt _____ C

11. 2 pt = _____ C

12. 3 gal 2 qt = ______ qt

13. 3 gal = ______ qt

14. 3 qt = ______ pt

15. 85 oz = _____ lb _______ oz

16. 8 yd 1 ft = ______ ft

17. 7 ft = ______ in

18. 48 in = ______ ft ______ in

19. 5 lb 0 oz = ______ oz

20. 8 C = _____ pt _____ C

21. 12 qt = ____ gal _____ qt

22. 4 ft = _____ yd _____ ft

23. 5 C = _____ qt ______ C

24. 3 C = _____ pt _____ C

25. 13 qt = ____ gal _____ qt

26. 10 C = _____ qt _____ C

27. 2 gal 3 qt = _____ qt

28. 4 qt = _____ pt

29. 3 lb 8 oz = _______ oz

30. 2 qt = _____ C

31. 4 qt = _____ C

32. 4 pt = _____ qt _____ pt

33. 2 pt = _____ qt _____ pt

34. 3 pt = _____ qt _____ pt

35. 12 C = _____ qt _____ C

36. 5 yd 1 ft = ______ ft

37. 4 lb 11 oz = ________ oz

38. 2 gal = ______ qt

39. 93 in = ______ ft ______ in

40. 32 ft = _____ yd _____ ft

41. 7 ft 10 in = ______ in

42. 9 C = _____ qt _____ C

43. 3 yd 2 ft = ______ ft

44. 5 yd = ______ ft

45. 2 C = _____ pt _____ C

46. 7 pt = _____ qt _____ pt

47. 2 lb 6 oz = ________ oz

48. 4 ft 5 in = _______ in

49. 35 in = ______ ft ______ in

50. 2 qt 2 C = ______ C

Metric Units

1 m = 1,000,000 microns	1 hectare (ha) = 10,000 m^2
1 m = 1000 mm	1 kg = 1000 g
1 m = 100 cm	1 g = 1000 mg
1 m = 10 dm	1 kL = 1000 L
1 km = 1000 m	1 L = 1000 mL
1 cm = 10 mm	1 cm^3 = 1 mL
	1 m^3 = 1000 L

1. 904 cm = ____ m ____ cm

2. 482 cm = ____ m ____ cm

3. 7 m 33 cm = ______ cm

4. 28 cm 2 mm = ______ mm

5. 5,610 ml = ____ L __________ ml

6. 1 L 600 ml = ________ ml

7. 867 mm = ____ cm ____ mm

8. 1 m 51 cm = ______ cm

9. 387 mm = ____ cm ____ mm

10. 4,040 ml = ____ L ________ ml

11. 3 L 260 ml = ________ ml

12. 5 L 20 ml = ________ ml

13. 357 cm = ____ m ____ cm

14. 7 m 32 cm = ______ cm

15. 441 mm = ____ cm ____ mm

16. 5 kg 950 g = ________ g

17. 854 cm = ____ m ____ cm

18. 7,140 ml = ____ L ________ ml

19. 800 cm = ____ m ____ cm

20. 837 mm = ____ cm ____ mm

21. 54 mm = ____ cm ____ mm

22. 7,360 g = ____ kg ______ g

23. 4 L 160 ml = ________ ml

24. 4 kg 660 g = ________ g

25. 7,630 ml = ____ L ________ ml

26. 3,040 ml = ____ L __________ ml

27. 7 L 600 ml = __________ ml

28. 1,170 g = ____ kg ________ g

29. 6 L 860 ml = __________ ml

30. 2,880 g = ____ kg ________ g

31. 2,440 g = ____ kg ________ g

32. 734 mm = ____ cm ____ mm

33. 8 L 110 ml = __________ ml

34. 1,310 g = ____ kg ________ g

35. 58 cm 3 mm = ______ mm

36. 2,210 ml = ____ L ________ ml

37. 837 cm = ____ m ____ cm

38. 5 L 560 ml = ________ ml

39. 8 L 340 ml = ________ ml

40. 64 cm 7 mm = ______ mm

41. 50 cm 2 mm = ______ mm

42. 557 cm = ____ m ____ cm

43. 2 L 510 ml = ________ ml

44. 507 mm = ____ cm ____ mm

45. 7,560 ml = ____ L ________ ml

46. 2,480 g = ____ kg _______ g

47. 9,820 g = ____ kg _______ g

48. 3 m 96 cm = ______ cm

49. 772 mm = ____ cm ____ mm

50. 76 cm 6 mm = ______ mm

ANSWERS

CUSTOMARY UNITS

1. 2 ft 6 in
2. 8 qt
3. 3 ft 4 in
4. 35 ft
5. 15 C
6. 1 qt 1 C
7. 1 qt 1 pt
8. 2 lb 0 oz
9. 2 qt 1 pt
10. 3 pt 1 C
11. 4 C
12. 14 qt
13. 12 qt
14. 6 pt
15. 5 lb 5 oz
16. 25 ft
17. 84 in
18. 4 ft
19. 80 oz
20. 4 pt
21. 3 gal
22. 1 yd 1 ft
23. 1 qt 1 C
24. 1 pt 1 C

25. 3 gal 1 qt
26. 2 qt 2 C
27. 11 qt
28. 8 pt
29. 56 oz
30. 8 C
31. 16 C
32. 2 qt
33. 1 qt
34. 1 qt 1 pt
35. 3 qt
36. 16 ft
37. 75 oz
38. 8 qt
39. 7 ft 9 in
40. 10 yd 2 ft
41. 94 in
42. 2 qt 1 C
43. 11 ft
44. 15 ft
45. 1 pt
46. 3 qt 1 pt
47. 38 oz
48. 53 in
49. 2 ft 11 in
50. 10 C

METRIC UNITS

1. 9 m 4 cm
2. 4 m 82 cm
3. 733 cm
4. 282 mm
5. 5 L 610 ml
6. 1,600 ml
7. 86 cm 7 mm
8. 151 cm
9. 38 cm 7 mm
10. 4 L 40 ml
11. 3,260 ml
12. 5,020 ml
13. 3 m 57 cm
14. 732 cm
15. 44 cm 1 mm
16. 5,950 g
17. 8 m 54 cm
18. 7 L 140 ml
19. 8 m 0 cm
20. 83 cm 7 mm
21. 5 cm 4 mm
22. 7 kg 360 g
23. 4,160 ml
24. 4,660 g

25. 7 L 630 ml
26. 3 L 40 ml
27. 7,600 ml
28. 1 kg 170 g
29. 6,860 ml
30. 2 kg 880 g
31. 2 kg 440 g
32. 73 cm 4 mm
33. 8,110 ml
34. 1 kg 310 g
35. 583 mm
36. 2 L 210 ml
37. 8 m 37 cm
38. 5,560 ml
39. 8,340 ml
40. 647 mm
41. 502 mm
42. 5 m 57 cm
43. 2,510 ml
44. 50 cm 7 mm
45. 7 L 560 ml
46. 2 kg 480 g
47. 9 kg 820 g
48. 396 cm
49. 77 cm 2 mm
50. 766 mm

www.ingramcontent.com/pod-product-compliance
Lightning Source LLC
LaVergne TN
LVHW060627170826
845677LV00027B/1767

9798869454799